MW01094113

BRAM STOKER'S DRACULA

RED

by Chase Berggrun

BIRDS, LLC | MINNEAPOLIS, NEW YORK, RALEIGH

Birds, LLC
Minneapolis, New York, Raleigh
www.birdsllc.com

Cover designed by Zoe Norvell
Interior designed by Michael Newton

Library of Congress Cataloging-in-Publication Data:
Berggrun, Chase
R E D/Chase Berggrun
Library of Congress Control Number: 2018932238

First Edition, 2018
ISBN- 978-0-9914298-8-2
Printed in the United States of America

CONTENTS

A Note on Process

R E D consists of twenty-seven erasure poems. They were produced using a system of formal constraints: text was erased while preserving the word order of the original source, with no words altered or added, according to a strict set of self-imposed rules. The poems use as a source the novel *Dracula* by Bram Stoker.

As the text of *Dracula*, a classic Victorian-era horror novel soaked with a disdain of femininity and the misogyny of its time, is erased, a new story is told, in which its narrator takes back the agency stolen from her predecessors.

This work was written at the same time its author had begun their own gender transition. As they were discovering and attempting to define their own womanhood, the narrator of these poems traveled alongside them.

CHAPTER I

I was thirsty

I was a country of queer force

rushing east to see the strangest side of twilight

I was a woman   in the usual way

I had no language   but distress and duty

I have been taught to doubt my mother and fear tradition

but my queer tongue   would not   could not shut up

The afternoon sun seemed mighty

and touched my arm with a delicate pain

A woman   kneeling in self-surrender to the new

weeping silver into great masses of greyness   the clouds

which ceaselessly walk and pause as though unmercifully urged on

Through the darkness I could see a stormy sea

a strange mixture of movements

Something slight and flickering seemed to mock my universal yes

I asked what this all meant

I struck a match

and its flame somewhere far off in the distance plunged

Suddenly a faint and endless absence

began beetling around

the howl that swept

the ruined sky

CHAPTER II

I must have been asleep

I must have been held in his trap

I did not know what to do

I waited in that nightmare

I heard a heavy sound   a noise of long disuse

A tall man   clad in courtly gesture

his cold face threw open a hollow roar inside me

He was charming   full of manhood

His mouth was cruel

the lips conceal a sea of wonders

I did not ask permission

I found a sort of library   littered with the history of death

I have come alone to learn about invaders

old days   when women waited their destruction in undiscovered places

I began to manifest my wishes

in the shrillness of the written day

I began to get diffuse and feel uneasy

The living riot of uneasiness

trickling out of my magnificent heart

describes a prison

CHAPTER III

Let me begin with observation

My concern is with agency

I was satisfied with my body

My desire is my own

my smile   my own

I unsealed the seriousness of sound

Freedom melted in the weatherworn abyss

Some weird effect of shadow

could allow an opportunity to resist

I took pleasure in disobeying

I determined not to compose myself

I suppose I was not unchanged

I thought I felt desire kiss me with red lips

Never could I be a girl on her knees

I was a storm of a woman

transformed with red light

heaving an imperious voice

forward into the dimness

CHAPTER IV

I tried to undress a mystery

although I had been so forcibly splintered

My work and quarrel was gathering wrath

I admit that I pretended to fall in with his law

I could not expose my secret to his smoothest eye

He consumed every scrap and trace of me

I began a nebulous gambol

new shapes danced   half-remembered shapes   phantom shapes

which gradually materialised from my own bright silence

In my prison   I cried

I was a woman against a monster

All the violences

like a pent-up dam when liberated

fell from me   as a vaporous garment   dissolved in warmth

My threatened body is more desperate

inside it I made a discovery

it was furnished with odd things   but all of them were stained

Down I descended a tunnel-like passage

I made a discovery

hate awakened in me

A great orchestra unhooked the heavy chains of the body

I unlocked despair

I pulled and pulled at a happier evil

My own body

a banquet

ever-widening

a song sung by wheels and whips

a determined echo   hammering away

CHAPTER V

There is nothing handsome about power

He says that I afford him a curious study

he loves undressing my ideas

Some girls must keep secrets

A woman ought to tell her husband very little

I wanted him blotted out

He seems to suppose that women were made to amuse him

He took my hand in his mistake

He couldn't help feeling a sort of manly fervour

Why are men so little worthy of a girl

CHAPTER VI

I was looking sweetly pretty

I think I fell in love with my own ghost

Everybody in the place knows

I was just a little heart-sick

I am sad

I see scattered all over the town a black clatter of waltz

I sometimes imagine myself a very sad spider

always growing   then partially diminished

progressing and undeveloped

I was spreading out again

I had been very sick   sleep buzzing about my brain

I shall invent a new life

it seems only yesterday my whole life ended

In sleep I walk along the edges of cliffs   then suddenly fall over

I sympathise with the weather   so perpetually nervous

I pray it will get easier   I pray for patience

A grey sunburst is tumbling in over the sandy flats

The sea sounds like some dark figure making straight for me

I'm afraid the dead remember dying

I don't want to die

I can't refuse to answer death

but it's in the sea

In that wind

the queerest storm coming

CHAPTER VII

The body of the storm   had a sultry heat

and a foreign foolhardiness

Strong men clung with ghostly effort

to their trembling experiments

swept away   by her impossible speed

She was sea-fog

a mass of dank mist the organ of her shudder

Unsteered by the hand of a man

crashing down on the eastern side

of some sudden emotion

She took all men   into blue water   *cum grano*

We finished fresh

Dawn entered Bosphorus   dissatisfied but steady

A rain-storm began to scowl

a maelstrom   a tempest   another tragedy

Only God can guide us in the fog

and God seems to have deserted us

The storm was sharp   she dressed herself in her intention

in sunbright foam like snow   she was restless at night

she is quite odd   she will admit

she had a look that men said   made them shudder

She was angry   howling harshly   eyes savage   hair bristling

quivering and super-sensitive

The whole agglomeration of things

furious and now in terror

will all afford material for her dreams

CHAPTER VIII

Tired   I walk towards everything except fear

over seaweed-covered rocks

I think that someday some new women

will be allowed to see each other happy

happy more than usual

I looked in all the other open rooms of my heart

A vague fear obscured the whole scene into a diorama of ruin

As sharp as a sword-cut   the light struck   a half-reclining cloud

Time and distance trembled in my body

To become in love with everything *apropos* of nothing

To see without seeming to stare

To change in the reflection

To appear peculiar

We never refer to sadness

as something that looks

like secrecy

but it does

I drifted on the fresh breeze

I did not like it

Joy   joy   joy   although not joy   a bad thing

I can feel it wet against my bosom

My journey is mapped and ready

I am only taking one dress

I don't want to talk   of infinitesimal distinctions

between man and man   see no difference   between men and maidens

I am the modern Morpheus
I made the minutes disappear
I am thin
an errant swarm of bees
a naked lunatic
faithful
selfish
old
a tiger
immensely strong
a wild beast
a paroxysm of rage
mercy
murder
coming
coming
coming

CHAPTER IX

I can hardly recall the journey

My thin pale dignity

has vanished

a wreck of itself

I have fallen in love with whispering

I want to be alone

I want to share my bitter hours   recorded here

I have given up sleep

I am getting fat   he tells me

that he loves me   but I doubt that

There he is   calling to me

There are spells of cessation from his passion

he was perpetually violent   suffused with distrust

furtively hurting me at night

I wish I could escape the bird-cage

The spells of quietness last a few hours each day

I enjoy the relief   even   appreciate it

Once   he became furious   and tried to kill me

He said there must be something wrong with me

getting worse every day

the fatal disease   of the girl-mind

                    I am distracted
                    I am filled with anxiety
                    I have a functional malady

I have no doubt

he took advantage of my confidence

I was broken by obedience

His arbitrary temper

all-embracing

once the poison of his pleasure has gone out of him

He must be angry with me because I am a girl

His geniality could merge into reality with a snapped finger

He never fails to remind me

that young ladies   do not ask questions

not a word

One outburst was unusual and so violent

his screams were appalling

I found my hands full of sound

When he apologised

I thought it well to humour him

He is reaping a harvest of lies

eating them like little crumbs of sugar

CHAPTER X

My Art   is a thing concerning sudden death

I shall unfold   when ripened

dig and sow and sprout

sprout   begin to swell

Change gathers round a foreign body

an envelope of ordered selfishness

I used my knowledge of this rule to recognise

the origin of my silence

I choke on a narcotic kiss

Something like life seemed to strain my soft voice

betraying emotion not at all wholesome

It once occurred to me that this was loss

but I abandoned this idea

drenched to a scarlet with want

Sleep   a presage of horror

Dread all night long rose and fell with the regularity of a pendulum

I was anxious about my work

my brain was beginning to argue with itself

I heard the low hiss of inspiration

My iron face was drawn and ashen

as a corpse after prolonged illness

I must obey

and silence is a part of obedience

Obedience   is grotesque to me

It keeps me fixed to weakness

CHAPTER XI

The wolf was a well-behaved wolf

but you can't trust wolves

The wolf had a cold look

as if upset at something

I did not like the insolent smile

a mouth full of white teeth

My own belief was that the wolf is simply an elaborate dog

In real life a wolf is a low creature

green eyes shining out of the dark

If he can't get food he's bound to butcher something tender

Satisfied   fatted with passion

a knife in his hand

licking up the blood

I went to bed   and fell asleep   I was waked

I was afraid   I tried to sleep   but could not

then came to me   the fear of sleep

I did not want to be alone   I was afraid   I heard a howl

I went back to bed   to go to sleep   I was not asleep

I was uneasy   I was startled   a little frightened

A gaunt grey wolf   clutched wildly at my neck

For a second or two   there was strange lightning

Time did not seem long but very very awful   somewhere near the
dogs all round the neighborhood were singing   I was stupid with
pain   the sound seemed like the voice of my dead mother come
back to me   I screamed out   the body of my dear mother flew
open for an instant and closed again   I laid flowers on my dear
mother's breast   my heart sank   I cannot leave   I am alone
alone with the dead   I can hear the low howl of the wolf   my
dear mother   gone

CHAPTER XII

How shall I describe the wound

I was only a young girl   I cried and sobbed

hysterical   I would not talk

There was no place for me   I see no light in life

To be unconscious was as bad as blind obedience

to the etiquette of death which governs a girl's life

Exhausted   I am exhausted

I cried   I cried

The best thing on this earth is a woman

God sends us men when we want other satisfaction

My girl blood   my queer blood   seemed to keep breaking down

The secret of my body   coming out

A series of little shudders scattering my strength

the difference between sleeping and dying

In the afternoon the sun was simply choking

I perform duty with all the moods and tenses of the verb

In accordance with the way of a wild beast

I could make men fear the same violent promises they made me

Forgive me   I am the angel of death

I do not speak   sleep stertorously

In the dim   some trick of the light moved uneasily

a sort of flapping moonlight   attracted by my struggle

the sissing indraw of light

almost touching me

At the edge of sleep I buried grief

I whispered with a tired child's voice

I hurled across the room my rage   like a shadow

faint   but with untellable pathos

sobbing in a way that nearly broke me

Change had come

Death had given back part of her beauty

it was as if Death might be dying

I stood and said   is it the end

when I asked   she only answered

Wait and see

CHAPTER XIII

I was undressing in my room when he entered

and began

to autopsy   operate   cut   unscrew

mutilate my tenderness

He had stolen so much

He pointed out that regarding matrimonial alliance

I had no alternative but to accept

This was my great tragedy

There was a mortuary air about him

his stalwart manhood seemed to have shrunk somewhat

a bitter blow to him

He threw his arms round my shoulders

his hand   tightening   trembling

I assured him that it was a moment that often happened to men

He was at a loss for words   and remembered violence

his property   to deal with as one would old flowers

Now   married to his interest

he was my husband   and didn't care if I was hurt

I am always anxious

His eyes seemed hard and cruel and sensual

he looked so fierce and nasty

as if he did not know me

he kept staring   his eyes fixed in the same direction

I feared to ask him any questions

so I remained silent

After a few minutes staring at nothing he woke up

he had evidently forgotten this dark episode

CHAPTER XIV

After a bad night I lock myself in my room and read

I had only imagination

I remember how on our wedding day   he said

I shall never let trouble or nervousness concern you   you can trust me

I must not forgive   I cannot

I know the real truth now

My imagination tinges everything with ill adventure

I suppose a cry clears the air   as other rain does

I have a good memory for details

it is not always so with young ladies   or so it had been said to me

I cannot comprehend this husband

Women all their lives are interrupted   considered hysterical

summoned to make children for the strong and manly

and for his sake must smile and not speak

Now this man I began to think a weak fool

I had trusted him   my husband

even half believed his words when he said

I would have an ordinary life   without dread

Let me tell you from experience of men

his brain and heart are terrible things

This man   impotent in the dark

He succeeded in getting me to doubt

everything took a hue of unreality

I did not trust even my own senses

You don't know what it is to doubt everything   even yourself

I am a wife he fashioned by his own hand

to be sweet and earnest and so kind

An idea struck me

Following great loss   people see things that others cannot

Men want to explain explain explain

see themselves new   pretend to be young

Ladies' bodies are deemed unholy

by the very men who burn them

Generations of men believe that women

walk amongst them without knowledge

My thesis is this

I want to believe   to believe

to believe in

a universe   willing

to understand

CHAPTER XV

I was surprised when unconsciously I imagined

the way his sperm dropped in white patches

which congealed as it touched my body

I felt lonely   I was chilled and unnerved and angry with myself

I thought I had found some distance away from that horrid reality

I realised the perils of a woman who spoke with hostility

not ashamed   not silent   my silence died

when it began to dawn on me

I was accepting the idea of this bloody work

It made me shudder to think of the woman he made me

buried alive by dreams

I know I must pass through bitter waters to reach to-morrow

I am young and desperate

If I have to I will burn the world

I start out lurid before outrage
I unhinged explanation from its frame
without permission
without endorsement
I violate limitation
and I condemn
the desecration of my body
I shall not give my consent

to anything more
I shall render an account
of a long life of acts
which were often not pleasant
and I will wipe away
this sorrow

CHAPTER XVI

My sweetness turned
to adamantine cruelty
purity to wantonness
obedient to nothing
an angry snarl
the remnant of my love
passed into savage delight
eyes blazed unholy
callous as a devil
growling as a dog growls
a cold-blooded groan
a languorous grace distorted
as livid as Medusa's
lovely blood-stained mask

Between the sacred closing of my knees

the place where the dead remain

where I in mourning wore the weight of the body

The career of this unhappy lady is just begun

instead of assimilating

I will strike the blow that sets me free

Amongst the silence of the stars

amongst infinite unholy snows

I will rejoice

I had more human considerations to look towards

Pain and waste were dear to me   a grinning devil now

And now   to find the author of this sorrow and stamp him out

and to the bitter end   I shall be ready

CHAPTER XVII

I was a sweet-faced dainty-looking girl

I knew how to repress a shudder

I tidied myself

I knocked at the door to surprise

I was trying to invent an excuse   in a different voice

I gave myself away to my typewriter

I have typed every thought of my heart

My power   to tell the other side

I have been touched by a wonderful anguish

I have tried to be useful

I have copied out the words of this terrible story

I contain no secrets

Stronger in the dark

I remain in the dark

A gleam of cruel metal

my only ray of light

Back when the world seemed full of good men

I remembered how to understand a narrative

    From my room within this deserted house

    I now trace carefully and with precision

        the shifting lines

        of liquid time

The future smelled like an old wound

I was sick with volcanic energy

It is true he would kill without pity

I came to the conclusion

that the best thing would be death

I had written the last hour   of his life

He covered his face with his hands

his voice walked quietly out of the room

Is there something in woman that makes a man feel free to break her

He grew quite hysterical   raising his open hands

beat his palms together

Women have something in us that makes us rise

I felt this big man on me and I thought

there was no woman whom he could know sympathy for

The sunshine was so fresh and comforting

impulsively I bent over and kissed him

choking his throat

quite calmly

CHAPTER XVIII

One time I tried to take human life

I tried to kill my own body   through prayer

I left behind   a brain

a brain that a man fashioned for me

determined to destroy this woman's nerve

I found in his absence a silence

like a blush-bright smile

I stretched my icy cold science
unfettered
by the limitations of tradition and superstition
I flourish and fatten and fly
as moonlight
as dust fused up with fire
in a world half free
I learned secrets
amongst mountains and graves
I dwell in barren data
I am at heart a horror
I sterilise the sunset with a bitter pill
a victim of manlike anxiety

The majority of men are full of air

I felt a strong impulse to release myself

in the direction of the negative

Can you not tell that I am militating against sullen acquiescence

Don't you know

that I am fighting to bring on the collapse of

quiet   well-bred   justice

CHAPTER XIX

This whole story is put together
in such a way that you know more than I do
but in a dreamy kind of way
so mixed up and earnest
wild sad and spiritual

At times
I tried to play with
the image conveyed
in the idea of our bodies

I could not get away from the feeling
that the feeling was common to us all

Some pain is too great for a woman to bear

to conceal from a world that will not even recognise her

that will simplify and reason   call it false delusion

He said my memory is a mental disease

I answered   I wish you would take your theories somewhere else

he sat indifferent to me

This world is no place for a woman in touch with her distress

drawn further into the fool wishes of men

sad and low-spirited   simply because they told me to be

Crying again   I must hide it   put a bold face on

I suppose it is one of the lessons that women have to learn

I can remember a queer stirring

a thin streak of slowness

across my thoughts

The man was loud   though I could not distinguish a word

he pulled my clothes over my head   he was bending over me

thought I was asleep   I was powerless

The heavy gaslight had grown thicker

It occurred to me   all his tricks and convenient smoke

thicker and thicker

Things began to whirl through my brain

and through it all came words   through fog

To unseat reason   fear would become woven into fear

I spent all yesterday trying to brighten   for I forgot how

He knew that if I was to flirt with power

I might want it

CHAPTER XX

I was not in a condition to prove much

hieroglyphical   half-obliterated

by booze and booze the night before

I am tired and pale

I kept a broken burden reticent

My dirty daily tasks   misled me

I found difficulty in discovering the right track

but had a vague idea of who to ask

I walked westward

beyond the framework still remaining

I would have given a good deal to gain access to dusk

autumn was closing in on me

I made a gallant effort to be cheerful

My task seems to have become repugnant to me

I had to get abreast of my own doubt

Through the cloudiness of insanity he dogged upon me

came inspiration and confidence

He would distract my attention with ridiculous nonsense

or with another homicidal fit

I cannot think clearly when my body is confined

and this story is haunted by

his lethargic buzz and fire

The only important observation was

men

are not

useful

I seem at last to be on track

to the coming destruction

the monster

his face on the floor

all covered in blood

CHAPTER XXI

A detail in a pool of blood

the body gathered in an awkward kink

I dress myself in easy anything

I softened into a swollen confusion

only slightly solid   I was shining

He beckoned

His hands   a dark mass like a thousand rats

A cloud closed over my eyes

I moistened myself with brandy

I held tight to life

I became like water

Kneeling on the edge of the bed   his face was turned

his left hand   held both arms   his right gripped

my neck   blood   a thin stream of it   his nostrils quivered

I lay in disarray

my eyes   and from them came   an endless moment

Cold moonshine dazed me   I began to pull on clothes

I drew back   unclean

Shame folded me like steel   tried to twist me in obedience

I could not feel the rise of reddening dawn

Silence   the sound of what happened

I want you to know all this

understand   how much I need to show you

It was he who caused me to disappear

My husband   my husband and other men

hunt me and command   my flesh my blood my brain

This is my pollution story

The eastern sky became clear
          as the awful narrative deepened
                    in the morning light
                              when the first red streak shot up my flesh

CHAPTER XXII

As I go mad   I write down   the little things

My mind is made of vague and desperate moments   all unspeakable

I have seen sand shake and shiver at the coming of the tide

I have taken measures to sterilise old sorrow

confined within the limitations of its envelope

So strange   how the despair became relaxed

I struggled hard to keep sight

of what was mine   the memory of that night

A scream   the white-hot fact of it

the overwrought echo of the scream

beautiful   unclean   unclean

I have written this under empty circumstances to attract less attention

my deserted condition produced a cold patient steadying

a plain conclusion

at last   I set out to destroy

CHAPTER XXIII

I threw grief-written lines all over my papers

I studied the necessity of no remorse

survived long centuries as an inmate

alone and hidden in the ground

I hastened towards the moment

I care for nothing now except brute action

It will take thousands of men to hold me back

I had been accustomed to obey

Now the old habit was just a nightmare

There was something so unhuman in

the snarl and stare that cut through the wide stream of my face

I love this wild beast in me

I was thinking of my appearance

my own sublime animal heat

and clung to hate

The word sounded like music

I will crush my husband in the folds of my dress

his night shall never end

My hate is drifting reefwards

sleeping in the softness of the sunset

Though I am weary

I must try to startle darkness

I must become an oblong disc of light

I must change my own sad dreaminess

to rigid red intention

Though I do not know what I am doing

though it may be too late

though danger on earth and under water

I must follow him to hell

CHAPTER XXIV

Where there is   where shall be
blood   blood   blood
soon   and   final
blood   blood
      where there might be
blood   a dense   blood
again   blood   again

My language was of blood
and full of movement
of fog   and morning far from fog
mouth made for speaking firm
the first forceful master of this monster form

Becoming
  wondrous
   geologic
    chemical
     magnetic
      electric
       and warlike

without aid from common men

I tasted enemy tongues to whet desire

to grow greater in the midst of greatest peril

I was still unclean

I still fear his poison

the power that compels my confidence to break

I will inflict a great campaign of preparations against the wolf

then hunt him hollow

I curved my shadows tenderly

I felt infected with trouble

a dreamless   maybe everlasting emotion

too great for human endurance

I go forth to flood him with agony

I fasten to a faith in steel

We are now drawing towards uneasiness

I am sure   some new end

CHAPTER XXV

Note this

I have come to understand   a particular freedom

without restraining mood

aglow   as if loosened

God   you are going to be so good to me

I know a poison you do not

beginning and ending with my hand

the blackest prelude

Note the quaint seriousness of my voice   low and strained

The flesh   the rough flinch

My fast-bending hand

which subdued the whiteness of his hair

I shrink into all wives   and their hands

their hands   that loved me best   I have not forgotten

that set me free   from the thrall   my husband held over me

What I have arranged to do will be no murder

Even if it were

I know now what men feel

that special excitement when in active danger

This necessary task   euthanasia   a comfort

I am in a fever of hands

I found him whetting

the edge of his throat   driven by cold

His hands instinctively sought

my smooth arrangement

He is sure I will come at his call

but I have not lost the grace a woman has

a power he may not take away

I   with perfect nervous poise

let loose wings   a thought-strong swan

When the time comes   I alone slaughter

I alone   ultimately triumph

The tight country he had tried to invade

he kissed it   sick and keen

There is more to tell and I shall tell you

Forgive me if I seem remorseless

selfishness frees my soul somewhat

Not even God is with me now

CHAPTER XXVI

This morning   the increasing swirl in his eyes

lying half asleep as he

distributed his guarantee   the routine hurt

this mixture of arousal and business

After a fog   I felt a wind carry through me

right or wrong didn't matter

I was rid of that type of punctuation

released from my promise to be grateful

to the man who invented this suffering

I have my conclusion

Memorandum

(*a*) He must be confined.
(*b*) A process of exclusions.
1. Endless difficulties in leaving.
(*x*) Investigate, hint, surmise: what might destroy him?
(*y*) Maybe.
(*z*) His highest fear, his victim.
2. It would have to be fatal.
3. The safest way: engulf him in water.
Firstly. A general plan of action.
Secondly. Ascertain his means of escape, and his suspicions.
His canniness has been proved before.

My husband's murder   required isolation
    in secret   I blotted out his traces
I have examined   ascended
    I read   the creaking sound
of his shaking hands   now
    at his most helpless   he is powerless

I took other precautions   I hunt well armed

It may be necessary to undo time   and re-incarnate

To destroy   I hesitate to write the word   destroy him

My legs are quick and lethal

I can fight   I can die

as well as men can

Fear shall find him near that fateful place

sad and tainted with illness   almost alive

in embryo   in a collapse of misery

I would take him into that place

There is work to be done before

I can escape those gloating lips

Forgive me   it is a dire need

I am giving   possibly   my life

I cannot sleep
how can I
it would be easier to die than to live
and quit before I start
dismiss the whole adventure

Here
as the cold seems to rise up and strike
it all comes home

CHAPTER XXVII

At full speed   he is hurrying towards me

fast   tireless

I wait firm   with a conqueror's instinct

All his heaviness in the air

and my hands get wilder

Low   the horizon   now

By morning

the patient daylight will guide

my unclean wrath

I saw the dawn with furs on

She became a hard neglected light

Not far off

the big yellow flood

at the end of the world

Her tender fire tethered to her smile

Hungry   and alone

Let me be accurate in everything
though you may at first think that I am mad
we are getting closer to a kind of carnival
fatal baptism
ancient and imperfect

I exulted
ere twilight
I could not eat
ever whiter the snow clung to me
a tremor
a test of the body
the scream tore at my hands
till the cold was quiet
snow came in flying wreaths
in the shape of women with trailing garments
then a sense of calm

The snow is falling lightly

far off I hear the howling mountains

I am sane   though proving it has been dreadful

I found my way

to where my work was roaring

in between his horns

Here   it was only death or freedom   the choice was easy

I have come to murder that man at last

A yearning seemed to clog the air

the open-eyed snow-stilled clarion

I braced   I dared not pause

I gathered the atoms of my sex to myself

Phantoms of emptiness spoke their dead selves through my butchery

I tremble and tremble all over in dissolution

screeching   writhing   fading

my whole body began to crumble

fixed in fervour   I was an illness fresh with fear

I go to meet him late in the afternoon
I go fast downhill and wrapped in cold
a perfect desolation far as I could see
I saw the cut of the sky in all its grandeur
a distant howling muffled in the snow
I joined him at the doorway
he took me by the hand
See   he said   here you will please me
he began

I was a high wind between flurries
he was lying like a black ribbon
I mounted his square chest
I felt imprisoned there
I saw him below me
he came quickly
a sudden cry from the south of me
he shouted in glee

I got out my revolver

It was strange to see the snow shining brightly around us

Every instant came in bursts

The hollow sound swept the air-space

It was hard to distinguish the real

as the sun dropped lower and lower

He was unaware at first

he fell forward in an unmistakable way

and gave a quick movement of his fist

I felt no fear but only a surging

In the midst of this the sun set

No time seemed to pass besides

By now the blood was spurting through his chest

his eyes glazed with the vindictive look I knew too well

As the moment plunged into my body

I sunk to the ground

Blood between my fingers

Red upon my face

My eyes followed the falling snow

And he died

ACKNOWLEDGEMENTS

This book is dedicated to survivors of rape, sexual abuse, and domestic violence.

First and foremost, I owe everything to Joe Gouveia.

My mother, Susan Russell, my grandmother, Marjorie Russell, and my whole family, Cole, Liam, Tom, and all the rest.

Antonina Palisano (the Nelly to my Paul), Catherine Pikula (my complaint wife), Dillon J. Welch (impatient inpatient), and Mark Cugini (sweetest spouse): my dearest hearts, my partners in art and war.

Matthew Rohrer, whose guidance and friendship helped me carry this book into the world.

The many incredible teachers I have had the honor of studying under: Martín Espada, John Murillo, Lisa Olstein, Rachel Zucker, Kimiko Hahn, Sharon Olds, Eileen Myles, Anne Carson, Edward Hirsch, and the entire faculty & staff of the NYU Creative Writing Program.

Nicholas Fuenzalida, Anna Meister, Morgan Parker, Emily Jungmin Yoon, Jayson Smith, Nina Puro, Natalie Eilbert, Bianca Stone, Ana Božičević, Wo Chan, Devereux Fortuna, Lauren Hilger, Mike Lala, Kamden Hilliard, Jerriod Avant, Joey de Jesus, Paige Taggart, Alexis Pope, Sarah Jean Grimm, Roberto Montes, Wendy Xu, Alexandria Hall, Carrie Lorig, Tess Crain, Linda Dolan, Tommy Pico, Stephen Ira, John Landry, Soren Stockman, Lauren Hunter, Phoebe Glick, Allyson Paty, Monica McClure, Dolan Morgan, Matt Nelson, Ben Pease, Lauren Roberts, Jaxin Niles, Stephanie Maclean, Radu Kolaric, Gerald Stern, Anne Marie Macari, Kaveh Akbar

Sampson Starkweather & the whole flock of Birds: Justin Marks, Chris Tonelli, Dan Boehl, & Matt Rasmussen, for their fierce love & dedication.

Excerpts from *R E D* have appeared, in different form, in *Barrelhouse*, the Lambda Literary Spotlight, *Powder Keg, inter|rupture, The Wanderer, Lemon Hound*, and *Menage*. Many thanks to the editors of those publications.

I was influenced by many, many different artworks during the making of this book, but these are a few of the most intimate & important:

Voyager, by Srikanth Reddy

the film *Nosferatu the Vampyre*,
written and directed by Werner Herzog

the television series *Buffy the Vampire Slayer*,
in particular Season 6

The Descent of Alette, by Alice Notley

Thanks to Wilhelmina Murray, Lucy Westenra, & "the weird sisters": the women of *Dracula*.

Final thanks to Bram Stoker, of course.

Chase Berggrun is a trans poet. They are the author of *R E D* (Birds, LLC, 2018). Their work has appeared in the Lambda Literary Spotlight, *Pinwheel*, PEN Poetry Series, *Sixth Finch, Diagram, The Offing, Beloit Poetry Journal*, and elsewhere. They received their MFA from New York University. They are poetry editor at *Big Lucks*.

"I tried to undress a mystery," testifies the speaker of R E D as this haunting literary performance—somewhere between neo-Gothic burlesque and formal experiment in queer auto-theory—begins. Erasing Bram Stoker's *Dracula* all the way down to its psychoanalytic minimalia, Chase Berggrun unearths a narrative not only of gender transition, but of the uncanny political and metaphysical transitions entailed by the metamorphosis of individual into chorus as well. By the end of this adventure in appropriation as self-disclosure, we learn that the "mystery" was self all along: "A detail in a pool of blood / the body gathered in an awkward kink / I dress myself in easy anything." Rapt and unsettled, we readers find ourselves, too, both saturated and implicated in the sanguinary affair of desire, "drenched to a scarlet with want."

> — SRIKANTH REDDY

"I violate limitation" says the speaker in Chase Berggrun's R E D and how can I help it, I love her to no end. This is a book that celebrates, no, reifies the power of erasure to usher in (re)creation. There are echoes of Hélène Cixous who, in *Coming to Writing*, says: "In the beginning, there is an end. Don't be afraid: it's your death that is dying. Then: all the beginnings. When you have come to the end, only then can beginning come to you." The gifts of transition. The gift of a body becoming "a determined echo hammering away." How my own body needed these "hands full of sound."

> — TC TOLBERT

Riot. Ruin. Storm. Fog. Smoke. Blood. Such words swirl and ravage and seduce the body, verb and noun in collusion with imperiled women. Chase Berggrun's R E D is deathy goddy girly queer erasure supreme. They turn the "I," that bossy mercurial pronoun, into a transcendent blade beyond confession. They take the broken thing of identity and endow it with the kind of agency that can only arise in the survivor, one who has seen madness only in what madness has already been done to them. The body queers, it splints, it is "afraid the dead remember," and it theories and plots behind the scaffolds of husbands and men. Here is a selfhood that comes alive in declarative flourishes, as it maps a redemption that is at times a most delightful physical texture ("I am only taking one dress") and at other times, damn near gnostic in its darkness ("Only God can guide us in the fog / and God seems to have deserted us"). If Sappho's fragments were the result of the fragile papyrus on which her poems were writ, then it is the fragility of men that has helped bless Chase with their miraculous tool of erasure. Chase's brilliant debut demands to be re[a]d with an exasperated, murderous clarity. Throw away the story you know about Dracula. Here it is real for the first time, in all of its chutzpah and necessary desecration: "Women have something in us that makes us rise." Amen, amen.

> — NATALIE EILBERT

CHAPTER XXI

a detail   in

a   pool of blood

the

body

gathered

in an awkward kink

I

dress myself.   in

easy

anything

I

have

typed
every thought of my   heart

my power

to

tell   the other
side

I

have

been   touched   by   a
wonderful
        anguish

    I have tried to be useful I have copied out the words

                of the terrible story

    I

contain

                                no secrets